# Bereshit

## Satan God. Angel

BY NORA GODDESS

DORRANCE
PUBLISHING CO
EST. 1920
PITTSBURGH, PENNSYLVANIA 15238

Dorrance publishing co
585 alpha drive
Pittsburgh, pa 15238
Visit our website at *www.dorrancebookstore.com*

ISBN: 979-8-8868-3136-8
EISBN: 979-8-8868-3995-1

# Bereshit

## Satan God. Angel

# The Introduction

This book is designed to defend Satan. God, the white angel, invisible deity who walks on Earth as man, means the spirit of God walks within me separately. I would like to introduce myself. I am the dark angel ruler of the entire universe. I am the living God. In past times, many believed in demons and aliens, yet no man has ever validated any of these information. I am the black angel and I give you the moon, the night, and death, among other earthly and holy things. Satan God is the light. He wakes you up in the morning and I put you to sleep at night. There is no such person as a devil, but a person can do devilish things to himself or others. Devil is an action, not a person, place, or things. It is a big holy lie. There is a building that is considered Hell, but it is here on Earth. When man goes to his long home, he may stay on Earth or enter a large building with extremely hot furnace with blazing fire, and when it is opening, it has a loud, rusty, creaky sound. When the door shuts, you hear the echoes from the heavy door that leads to the incinerator, and thou shall burn an eternal burn, depending on what you have done on Earth which will be revealed to God through your spirit that sits at the base of your spine called the Holy Ghost. He is not Satan Himself to show ownership that Satan God is the father of man. There is a myth about the Holy Ghost, that He is a dove and Jesus is in your heart. There has been misinformation about the 666, the so-called sign of the devil. The 666 was made up through the Indian nation to bring fear in the lives of the reader, and to reduce man to uncivilized thinking as the Indians did in those days. Some think uncivilized in modern days due to misinformation from their spirits that they never saw again, but still claim demon in reference to God, yet they do evil through the Holy Ghost whom they call the kundalini. The Indians made the world believe they were so knowledgeable about the kundalini that they have performed rituals that have ruined the lives of millions on Earth. They do not know who God is, if so they would not be performing evil acts to raise the spirit of God up, which is very dangerous. This act that the Indians used is a deadly act and it may not be forgiven. To use witch-craft and other rituals to entice God can kill you. The spirit is not supposed to be released until after death. Many people have ruined lives by doing witchcraft on the person. The person who has the spirit in this fashion has many issues. The first issue is, they did not know God, so you are praying to who? Jesus, the myth? If you are not praying to yourself, then who are you praying to? I only acknowledge religions who preach true reli-gion, not a myth of a god. I will acknowledge they that preach God and not the son but acknowledge the son. To honor a son and not the father is a damnation to your soul, for only I can save you from eternal destruction. I am the living God. The highest power in the world, the black angel Nora Goddess female deity, the living God representing the white angel Satan God, the invisible and supernatural angel. I came to call the world to order. And to release our sons who took God's name and cru-cified God's name, just to be adored by man while openly deceiving God. What good is a man if he gains the whole world and loses his soul, what good is that man? That man is good for the eternal flames which he shall enter at death, for his sins are great and they are many. The first son is in a bottomless pit; it has a bottom but he feels the pit. The last son is in eternal fire because his transgressions were greater than the first son. It has been 10,000 years and it is time to release them from bond so that they may rest in peace for all eternity, for they may never enter the gates of the mother and father, due to the centuries of destroying the father of the light name, and reduce his father to laughter, scrutiny, name-calling, belittlement of God the Father, praising the son and other gods, and denying the true god, who is the father of all on Earth. Respect instead they televise hate speeches on the media such as television, radio, church, books, and any document to tear down my god, a god unknown to man due to other myth gods, whom no one ever met in person but in dreams and visions. Man has drawn many pictures of the devil, yet no man knows who the devil is! Who is the devil? Man truly can be a devil; a devil would be an angel, the most powerful angel ruler of Heaven and Earth. There is a myth a good god and an evil god. The truth is the bible is about God and his sons. Satan God is the good god and his two sons are evil gods, but the sons wrote it to tear down their father's name so they could be praised and honored, and not God because God is invisible. Therefore, they utilized the abuse of power to tear down their father Satan God, the angel of light in their name. They end their prayer with the Egyptian god's name, Amen. The Egyptians have a mythological god that they pray to, but I am God and my word is law. Not even Satan comes before me, and he is my god. A prayer ending in their name is worthless and satisfy they that believe in their false God or gods. Any god that man thinks owns Planet Earth, tell him to come see me and please remind them to bring their armies, because I am not going anywhere and I will welcome you with swords of my tongue. The introduction of the decoding of the bible will reveal that the book is written in fairytales, but it is a story of Satan God and his sons. My name the most holiest name on Earth and the universe. It was never revealed in the bible that God had a wife, because my name means death and life. I own everything in my world and there is no day of death; when I am ready to go home, I will go home to a place where no man, dead or alive, has ever been, and will never see, only in a dream. My name shall never be spoken out loud, for the word Nora speaks holiness. I am not Satan God's daughter or his experiment; I am above Satan God the deity, because I am the living God. I am God! This is the placement of the order of the world. The judges of Planet Earth are the highest power in human form. The military are we; we represent the military protection of each country. The infrastructure of the world includes the architect, contractors, and all forces who are responsible for the infrastructure of each country. People are the police; police are the people, because they are the protectors of the people in each country. All countries should be set up like this. No country can be run by civilians as they are now. That is why there are so many problems in the world due to the wrong meaning of a statement, which has the countries in an upside-down situation. I view the world as living biblical. When no nation should be run in a biblical fashion but live in holiness, because religion is a lifestyle which means different things to people. If man really cares about each other, then why is there hunger in the world? The reason there is hunger in the world is because food and water should be free to man, and paid for by the government using the people's money; instead, man is worried about skin color, grade of hair, and 400-year-old slavery. If slavery were so important to any nation, this act of slavery should not be tolerated in today's world. If religion is for humanity and civilization, then why do you see so many hungry people in my world? Instead of setting them up to take care of themselves, you offer them free items and it continues indefinitely. This act of enabling has cause man to suffer. Throughout the world, man is suffering due to countries depending on another country to support or need aide for them, making them a slave to another country. I see the USA as parents to the world, yet they are not acknowledged but criticized for doing good, criticized for doing bad, and just criticized for the sake of conversation. The problem that I see is people don't know their role in my world. First of all, you were born with feelings, and all other nerves were researched and practiced on you by scientists. Science is the tool of the operation of man, and the medical field is the healer of man; without them, you would be uneducated, uncivilized, and dumb with only sound. Without science, you would not be able to function because it is science who taught man how to use a very small percentage of his brain. Man uses over 30% but over 60% is untouched, but being reviewed by science until made perfect. The judges, the fathers of the world, control each country and the entire DCIS system, which is the foundation of the law. Nora Goddess is the ruler of Heaven and Earth. Satan God, my god, is father to all on Earth. I, Nora Goddess, am the Mother to all nations on Earth. The world has my features which is the tigerish/cattish appearance. There is a misunderstanding about religion and spirituality. Religion is a lifestyle that is agreed upon and practiced. Spirituality is who a person is. Through spirituality, the only active nerve that is recognized in the human race is feelings, because emotions are what you learned and practiced. Feelings are deeper than emotions, because feelings are how the brain operates. Take, for example, it is said that a narcissist has no feelings and doesn't care about anyone; this is false information. Everyone is born a narcissist because you don't know anything. Man is taught how to do things by the advice of science and doctors, but man needs to learn how to program his own brain by learning new things and new ideas. Let's take, for example, there are so many people suffering financially and they don't have a way out. There is a way out. The DSS have people all over the world who need someone to care for them, and the government will pay you a great income to help the world. There are many programs that need affordable living that you can utilize to help others. The military has thousands of misplaced service members who need affordable housing. There are many state and government jobs to be filled, and your help would be greatly appreciated. Another program you can offer others is to make your house pay you. Rent rooms out in the empty-nest homes and instead of downsizing, now you can start over. Why live great while you are younger and claim poverty or helplessness in our golden age? Live until you die, not die while you live.

# Childbirth

A baby is supposed to come into the world unscathed and untouched, meaning a c-section. The reason a c-section is the proper method of birth is to control the amount of children a woman can have; it also eliminates poverty, and eliminates severe birth defects by not forcing an entire human being through a small opening, causing their soft bones to become damaged during birthing. Often, the nerves in the man\brain is damage. Let's take a look at this childbirth situation. A child grows in the uterus and then the child is ready for the world through vaginal birth. First of all, the opening is too small to bring a child into the world without causing damage due to the squeezing and pressing of the hard bones of the mother to force the child out,9 causing great pain and even death. Even though the bones are soft, some nerves and tissues become damaged during the birthing process. The bones will become hard as the child grows, but many parts will not develop properly. With a c-section, the child is taken directly from their house, the uterus. With this birth, the birth is a normal birth. Why would God let animals and beasts give birth to their offspring without screaming and hollering, while a woman is in great pain in delivering a child in vaginal birth? This abuse is taught as a punishment from God to a woman because of the bible. It is written that Adam and Eve shall suffer through hard labor and a painful birth. It is implied that God has mercy on an animals or beasts, but not for a human being in the image of God. You suffer through childbirth because women are having children in a fashion that is for animals; that is why the world is over-populated due to the incorrect way of delivering a baby. If there were a study on the difference in the behavior of the vaginal birth children verses the c-section, you would find their feelings are different and so are their characters. Man is brain; he is perfect and perfected to a god through studying the brain and developing a unique life by learning how to operate your brain. Through science, man has lived his life based on the findings in science. Through spirituality you can heal yourself, but you must know which nerve feeling to use in order to get the best results. In the supernatural studies, they are studying the ultimate task of living in this world in harmony and being civilized in dealing with each other. If you can reinvent man by using the body parts of the deceased to replace damaged body parts. If the body dies, the brain can still live, but if the man/brain dies, life is over. Death is inevitable; why worry about it? Just live until you die. Many people in the black and white nation are passive aggressive. The reason so many people suffer from this is due to the American welcome smile to show you are friendly. This is a great tactic, but it teaches a person how to deceive another person with a smile, and this tactic of smiling without a reason is a sign of dishonesty in many nations. The blacks smile more than the whites to show others that they are friendly. Some blacks are so used to living this lie, that many blacks have a permanent grin on their faces, and it concerns me. Nobody is happy, all the time not even a monkey. If you learn to control this passive aggressive behavior, you will be able to control oneself. A passive aggressive person has serious issues, and they don't know it. There are many self-help books out there, but if a therapist is available, they would be more suitable for you, because you must remember as Christians and Catholics, you are passive aggressive due to your misunderstanding of the teaching of the bible. Anyone who lives through the bible is living a lie. The bible has made many people who are wolves in sheep clothing, meaning smiling to deceive another person. The way the bible is written is not civilized, nor does it help humanity, yet as Christians and Catholics, you are very good at helping others. In fact, I praise you for all the great things you have done, yet it was done in vain, because if it were blessed, poverty would be fixed. Man has defeated himself by not caring for himself first, but caring for others more than he cares for himself, because many were taught to give your last if someone needs it. Many religious people are living a lie; they help others and are sitting in their homes hungry and broke, but giving to others to show you care. In reality, you care for others more than you care for yourself, and this makes a person aloft with himself, which is abuse of thy self. Why would you give someone your last when the last is all you have? If you do this act, it means you don't love yourself as much as you love others. The bible and its contents have ruined the lives of many by choice. Many people know Jesus is a myth, but they have been lying so long that it hurts them to seek the truth, because a lie does not hurt. It only hides a person.

# Who is Nora Goddess?

**Supernatural Being**

I was born Nora Lee Holmes in South Carolina on February 15th, 1959. I came in with a hurricane and almost died at birth. I came from a religious family; both of my parents were gifted. My mother was a dream interpreter. My father was a genius. I was born with the Holy Ghost awakening to return to Earth, to become Satan God's wife in the law, which was performed by the signing of my given name, Goddess, by Judge William S. Mooney, and signed by the clerk of assignment Susan Nespoli at Portsmouth Circuit Court in Portsmouth, Virginia. I also came to tell man who he is and his purposes on Earth, and to rebuild Planet Earth by destroying the volcanos, so that more land can be obtained for your pleasures by adding height to the land. We are here to give you the correct instructions on building on the land. The land must be logged first, then prepared for traveling. All haunted houses on Planet Earth should be burned to the ground instead of destroyed by other means, due to the nature of spirits living among the living being. Burning of the building is an insult to the spirit, and it lets them know they are no longer welcome, and this is no longer their home. Spirit forces deals with climate changes. Spirits have energy, but not the energy they had while in this life, but their energies can affect the weather. In order to change the climate, man must discontinue bad usage of the land and its inhabitant. I am also here to appoint nations to teach man how to operate the spirit, and to give scientific and medicinal information to remake man and find cures for old, unsolved diseases. I came also to help the archeologists find old places buried deep within the earth that are accessible. The grave hole of Yesshuraa' whom you call Jesus, is located in England in a hole approximately five feet deep. The site is located near a tree with unfamiliar symbols. These symbols are the symbols of Mary called DNA Yesshuraa' wife his oldest sister. Yesshuraa' walked on Earth as man; he is the nation of the British who also are the Americans, who are the first grandchildren of the world. The bible, the word, was started by

Yesshuraa', but was vandalized by man as time passed from centuries to centuries. The word devil, the 666, and many occult symbols were started in the Hindu religion, which used both spirituality and religion to govern themselves. The word devil is an action of the mind and can be a noun based on sentencing of a word. The many images that are pictured of God are fragmentations of the imagination of man in visions and dreams. There are many who have seen sightings, but many of them would tell you it happened just once, even though there have been different occurrences of seeing phantoms. There are many who believe in aliens, yet no man has ever seen one alien on Earth; if he did, he would treat them the same or worse than man treats the rulers of Heaven and Earth. Man mistreats God in his own home, and this shows man has no hospitality for God, so it is not expected that he will have so much respect for man, yet man treats each other in an uncivilized manner if its suits him at that time. A person's religion is a lifestyle and should not be confused with spirituality. How a man worships is his entitlement, but to destroy the name of God before the world is blasphemy. If man wanted to know who I am, he would ask me; instead, he makes movies and makes statements about who I am, when in fact the world does not know me at all. If the world cared about me, the world would try to know God, but the world wants to live in deception to protect themselves while being unworthy to God. There is not one person on Earth who loves Satan God more than me, so where are you? It tells me the world loves man more than God. That is witnessed by all that know that I am here on Earth with powers unseen by anyone on Earth. I am the dark angel, the highest power on Earth and in the universe. I am here with those who are in the dark to encourage them to walk in truth and to turn their lives around. I also destroy volcanoes. I can stop the forces of the earth. My powers are unmatched by any human on Earth, or heavenly angel or demons. Satan is the maker of man. All nations on earth are of Satan God, even the grandchildren through the son. The reason the Christians and the Catholics states that you must come through the son to get to the father is because they came indirectly from the father, so they pray to the son but only acknowledge the father. In some religions, it is stated that Jesus/Yesshuraa' is God; this is incorrect. He is the first son of God. There is nothing wrong with honoring their God, but it is an insult to belittle God. Yesshuraa' was called a devil, but he was not a devil; he used witchcraft to ward off demons and other spirits, and he was not a poor man, but a very rich man from England. He is in the genre of the singletons of England royalty. He invented witchcraft and other occults. God does not have to use voodoo or any magic; God is almighty and He is the power. The second nation of whites called the Jewish nation who have the different tones of white. The statement in the bible that says the first becomes last and the last becomes first. This statement means even though the son brought in the first nation, he is second to his father, so that is why the father nation comes before the nation of the son by status. No son is equal to his father, because the father made the son. Due to the situation of the father and son, the first white nation is the grandchildren of Satan God and Nora Goddess. For this reason, they are called the children of God. I will also show science how he can explore space in a different and unique way. I shall teach the occult world how to teach man to live in harmony on Earth, because you have seen some things in the land of death that you know are real. The reason my mother knew I was awakened is because she could feel the serpent moving around inside of me. Being a genius and the goddess comes with concealment, because I never wanted anyone to know I saw children who were similar to me were medically and psychologically abused, because man did not know that the serpent within all is the root of all good and evil; it is which deed that you feed will be the strongest. The reason I say abuse is because I used to see them do experiments on these children and give them medications that they used on a trial basis. Some children were placed in institutions because science did not and still is baffled by a genius/God. I am the goddess of the world. I am not of this world, but I was born into this life to execute the rights of this world that we know today as Planet Earth, but in the beginning, we are angels and are still angels. God is from the land of the dead. I am the living god. Worship is given to Satan, the father of man. Satan show ownership by evidence of the serpent lying dormant in most people, but awakens in some people, meaning he has physically possessed your body through the words you utter to God. There is no turning back. Once possessed, you will feel the movement of the spirit physically moving inside your body, 24 hours per day, seven days per week, and the more you feed God through utterance, the bigger the serpent becomes, so be careful what you offer the spirit or sacrifices made, because God will require this of you. It is you who makes the choice of do you want God to have part of you or all of you? If you give God all of you, you can never get you back, and one day you will want to return to the way you were, but it will never happen in this life ever again. So be careful what you ask for. If you give all of yourself, give it in goodness even though some may perceive it as evil due to not understanding the spiritual world. Through religious material and making things up, many lives have been ruined by the teaching of the bible and other books. The bible actually teaches hate and accepts emotional abuse that was written by man to abuse him emotionally. Why would man want another person to burn in an eternal hell? Why is man happy to see man fall from grace, lose money, and try all he can to ruin another person's life? The sad thing is people join in as gangs to take that person down and they have no regards for how he takes care of himself or his family, but are just so happy to see him suffer and left in poverty, then man says to each other. We are fair and we believe in treating each person in a civil way. Man says this because it is easier to pacify oneself.

In regard to man worshipping man, there is nothing wrong with it; there is nothing wrong with man worshipping other gods. Just know there is a higher God; in other words, never put anyone before Satan God. Due to my gifts and powers, I see things on a different fashion. Human beings have gifts and powers because man is supernatural in spirit.

# Trances of the Goddess

The golden gate bridge is a large bridge that shapes like a small n and falls into a slope at the bottom; that's when you walk a path to go to Heaven on Earth. The bridge has lights on both sides. The bridge is taller than any bridge on Earth. It has white sparkling stones with light gray stones, with silver matted expensive looking stones that are shiny, and sparkles like diamonds from one end of the bridge to the other. Its appearance is smooth in vision. The golden gate bridge has two lanes. One lane is larger with rocky roads, instead of a smooth pavement like the smaller bridge on the left. It is a narrow lane. This lane has fewer people traveling on it. On the narrow lane, they were walking in a normal pace, and they were joyful, and they respected each other while walking to Heaven on Earth. The right side of the bridge, just have regular road rocks, but the people on the right side of the bridge made a lot of loud noises and people were arguing, shoving, and mistreating each other.

# Pathway to Heaven

Here is one of my vision traveling experiences. My experience in this life on the golden gate bridge to Heaven. I was lying on my bed reading the bible, when suddenly I was in a trance. In the trance, I was on the narrow road on the golden gate bridge and my brother, who was my sibling that died at age 16, walked next to me. He was dressed in all black. He had on a black button-down shirt and a black Levi type jeans, and I did not look at his shoes because I did not hear his steps while we were walking. In my vision, I knew he was dead but I could not understand why he was on the bridge with me. My brother did not speak to me; he just walked with me. It was a long walk. I could see from a distance there was a large gate; as I got closer to the gate, it had six black sheep placed on the top of the gate bar, because the gate had six posts on one side and one post on the closing side where the latch was located. While we were walking, my brother began to run because the gate was beginning to close. He began to speak with me. He started running and he said, "Cindy, run! Hurry! The gate is going to close, hurry, Cindy!" The gate began to close, and my brother said, "Cindy, hurry, run, the gate is going to close." I tried to run as fast as I could, but I could not catch him. As he was running, he kept looking back. He only looked back three times. I started running even faster because I wanted to come with him. My brother had just got in before it closed, and he said to me while behind the gate, "Cindy, hurry! The gate is closing!" As I reached for the handle, I stretched my body and hands out, because the gate was almost shut. I figured if I could grab the handle, I could pull the gate back open, but as my right hand was grabbing at the gate, it shut. I heard and saw the gate shut. The closing of the gate was a medium click. Once the gate clicked, everything disappeared, and smoke mist clouds were seen. When the gate locked, my brother disappeared in the smoke like clouds. I suddenly came out of the trance and continued doing what I was doing.

The next trance was with my sibling during my pregnancy. One day I was lying in my bed with an orange polka dot maternity dress on, and suddenly I went into a trance. I was sitting on a silver metal locker bench, it was cool in the locker room, it was cold enough to have a jacket or light coat on. I did not have a jacket on, and I don't remember what I was wearing. I was sitting on a silver metal gray bench with my fingers mid-way locked together, because it was quite cool in the locker room. Suddenly, the door opened, and my brother walked into the room wearing the same color clothing he wore on the golden gate bridge: a black button-up shirt and black denim pants. I never saw his feet or shoes or heard any walking sounds. My brother sat next to me, but he did not speak. He looked into my eyes, but he did not speak. He looked as if he wanted to ask me something but I immediately said to him, "Theodore, you are dead," because my mother told me he was lonely and wanted company. My mother told me if he came back to me in a trance, tell him he was dead because he did not know he was dead. After I told my brother he was dead, his eyes widened, his mouth opened, then he stood up and looked at me in shock, and then I woke up. I never saw my brother in a trance or dream ever again. There is a misconception about Heaven and Hell. Heaven is the skies and Hell is beneath the earth, some say the grave. When a person dies, they remain where they died.

When you die, you do not leave the earth; you remain here on the land unseen. There are times when people have seen apparitions, but if you notice, they normally say it happened once or twice. Many people have a haunting due to the house or building. If there have been mass murders in a home or building it should be burned to the ground in order to remove the deceased in spirit from your home. If you tear the house down and rebuild in a place that had massive murders, they are still there walking around, and through mirrors they can enter your home, because to the dead, this is their home. Burning destroys the spirit and relieves the world of those negative vibes. There is no such place that you go where you will be walking around in robes and singing and dancing for God; this is a biblical, false statement. Whatever you did not do while living, you will not get a chance to do when you die. Many people say they can pray you into Heaven, how? Heaven is the sky. Many ghosthunters are fooling themselves because they cannot help the dead. This is a land that no man ever came back from. No man has a true vision of life after death, because there is life after death, but you will not be able to communicate with the living as you did while on Earth. It is a bad practice to disturb the dead unless you are me, Nora Goddess. Many religious organization claims God wears clothing and that God is rich. God is a spirit, and he does not wear clothing nor does God have money. I have money and I wear clothing, but not God; he can't be seen but felt. God does not have money, but he can show you how to make money, but you must want for yourself because nobody can make a person want anything. He has to want for himself in order to build his life and grow. It is amazing that you believe in the bible when it does not teach civilization, humanity, independence, but they do believe in begging for God, which is not what God wants. A beggar is just that: a beggar. It is amazing that the Christians and Catholics come in all colors, yet they can't get along. As the goddess of the world, a Christian goddess, the church violated me at five years old and they turned their backs on me for embracing the truth. In Catholicism and Christianity, they are followers, and many don't think for themselves; they need the minister, Pope, or other dignitaries to tell them what to do. They allow man to control them, but they can't seem to cure hunger and race. I told man where he came from; I told man a woman is not supposed to have vaginal births; I told the world Jesus is a myth because he never existed and this is all fairytale. I am the smartest person on Earth and I am also the strongest on Earth. This is my world, and I can prove it and have proven it. The maker of man is Satan God and Nora Goddess. If there is another god who rules our world, tell him to come and bring his army. Who and what I am is a mystery to you, and will remain a mystery because man has you thinking false ideas. Instead of asking me who and what I am, they assume false information. I have two hearts, one for me and the other for God, and this can be proven through the doctors. I have double of other parts in my organ system. I am a god, not an alien, or demon. I just said that to see your reactions; it's funny you believe in aliens, yet no one bother to ask me about aliens. There are no aliens in our world; they would be too afraid of Satan. Satan God said in the navy medical center before the entire medical staff through my mouth. God said he is not afraid of anyone on Earth and he stepped back and did a dance step in the emergency room of the naval hospital. In fact, they saw some things God did in me that baffled them. After seeing the doctor, by the way, they had military police officers in the room with me and outside of the door. After the examination, I was given his number to make another appointment, but when I called him to get another appointment he would not answer the phone nor did he return my call. A doctor would have to be prepared to examine me because it will be something they never seen before in any human being on Earth. The Christians and Catholics utterly disrespected us by trying to make me out of a liar when the world witnessed the truth in me. I will remember the Christians and the Catholics who mistreated us in our world all because they want the world to believe in a lie. As much praying as the Christians do, where is your so-called God? He does not exist in our world. Many blacks really do believe in the bible and truly live by it, in regards to being poor and begging for needed supplies that could easily be bought by that person. We have 12 sons in the first life, and we also have one in this life which can be verified.

# Who is Woman?

A woman is a complete body. All females are born with a full body, meaning a head and all other parts, including the holy ghost, which carries the male manhood, along with the heart of man, which is of the spirit. A woman's brain is unsettled due to her animal instinct brainwaves. A woman is solitary in nature, meaning she likes to be number one. She is also territorial and will defend what is hers from other females and males. Women camouflage their emotions to hide their true selves. Women hate each other but hate to admit it. They hate another woman for their facial features, shape, hair, clothing, material things, and even her mate. A woman will befriend another woman and take liberties with her husband, because in reality, she thinks she is better for him. Many women look at another woman's success and some become jealous of another woman's gains. In regard to gossiping with a women, don't gossip. They would rather destroy you, so you can lose all that you have, and then the laughs, tear down, and sabotaging of another person's life. In other words, many females are happy when another woman is poor. There is a saying beauty is skin deep. Many women use beauty to capture the hearts of men, and are happy to be his trophy wife or girlfriend, in order to live a luxurious lifestyle that he can afford with ease. Any woman who takes her beauty to be lauded by a man is foolish because the woman neglects her future, making her husband/boyfriend's future hers. A marriage like this can fail and cause havoc in the marriage if the husband decides to leave because he is tired of taking care of her, then what do you have?. If you did not prepare, you will have nothing other than what the court tells him to give you. Then you look in the mirror and realize beauty is only skin-deep, and if all you have to bring to the table is love and beauty, you will end up being hated or develop self-hate. All females should seek employment or start your own business. Why would any women want someone to take care of them as if they are kids? Why would any woman want a man without a job? Why would a woman assume that when she marries, all her troubles are over because you have a successful man that gives you the world? What this man should do is support your independence and enroll you back in school or an on the job training program, so she can bring in her share to support herself, so if a divorce is necessary, it would be a reasonable separation. No marriage should be forever because it forces many people to become fake people, which is a passive aggressive behavior. All marriage should have a five, ten, fifteen, and so forth contract, so when the home is gone you will have legal rights to your finances. All females should require up to $100,000.00 in loans before she marries a man; he will give it to her as a wedding gift, and this money is not for bills. This is your gift from the one who wants to make your house his home. If cash is a problem, then tell him to get credit, and if he has no money or credit but a job, let him go and tell him if he cares about a woman, he will put his financial house in order. If he is not loan-worthy, then don't marry him. He will be a problem. Don't make him believe you will wait on him; let him find someone else. You have seen some of his flaws so why take a chance on him because you claim you love him? What is love other than emotions that were manifested by you? The reason I say you is that most men don't love a woman like we love them. In many situations, the man is your boyfriend, and he does not know it, because he did not ask you to be his friend with a potential marriage proposal. There are many reasons a man should give his wife a gift, because she will be a gift to him through marriage. The subject of a marriage is both parties should have a career or a business so that they can be independent of each other, yet come together in marriage. If both have their own future plans, and there is a divorce, it can be a reasonable divorce with both parties in an agreement, and both parties win. Both can continue to design their future. This manner of divorce would be an ease, and all parties are fine, because you don't need each other, so therefore why stay in a marriage if the love is gone? Most women will not leave the cash and are waiting for him to die. There is a reason a woman responds in speech, but there are self-help programs that can correct the behavior of the beast-type behavior. The first and the most important is to tell yourself the truth. Is this really you or is this the fake you, which is an action that can hold you back because you don't want to face who you really are, thus never living to your full potential? You must be honest with yourself, which is very hard, because to master self is a very hard task. Self-management is one of the hardest feelings you will ever master. The reason you have not mastered this is because you did not know who you are or where you came from. To cure this problem, I shall go into details. What does unsettled mean? It means a lack of stability dealing in unresolved matters in your life ,not demanding a solution. That is why the same problems keep showing up, because they were never solved, only talked about. What is jealousy? It is an overwhelming feeling of insecurities. What does wild mean? It means unrestrained, undisciplined, and some act crazy, but are not crazy, they act crazy. What is betrayal? Betrayal is the breaking or a violation. Betrayal can cause someone to lose trust or confidence that produces moral and psychological conflict within a friendship or relations; betrayal is intended and treacherous. What is envy? It is a negative view of yourself to desire what someone else has. What is vicious? Vicious is an act intended to cause physical or mental harm. Many women are suffering major health problems due to being vicious in their thinking, which brought on the medical issues. What is beauty? Beauty is pleasure. In order to find the true self, one of the first things you must do is to correct these behaviors, or you will remain the same and never being all you can be in life. These negativities interfere with your daily living and they cause health issues. The reason there are so many problems in the world is because of woman. She has placed her nation in great danger. She dishonors her husband. Many do not operate their homes properly. They tear down each other's nations due to violation and vicious acts. Many women are the head of the house and make the husband the woman, thus taking on a role that can never be hers, because only a man has the actual god head; you have the god head secondary. Women has ruined the world with uncontrolled desires, and in some nations, a man is reduced to a slice of bread due to the disrespect of the women in that nation. Any nation of man that allows his goddesses to berate him before the world should stand up and defend their titles. If they don't respect you, place a gag order on them, because you are the god head, not her. Woman will find peace after all of these corrections have been made. I will guarantee you, you will see a better world. I can guarantee you without man there is no life, and without God, there is no man. These violations do not mean all women do these things, but in order for a woman to regain respect from a man, you must change your feelings because your emotions are what made you the way you are. You were born with feelings, not emotions. God helps those who help themselves. Help is available through self-help or counseling, but you and only you can make that call. Some people say I have been like this all my life and I am not going to change. If you remain the same all your life, you will never grow. You may grow rich, but you will not grow rich as a person. Take inventory of yourselves and learn to love you as a woman first, because how I see it; you love the man more than yourself. A man is a brain/head; he will change and will not hesitate to leave you if he knows it is a better life ahead for him. A man will not let you take his future; he would rather leave you or compromise with you. A man will not love you with all of his heart, because his heart is of God. That is why no matter how much he loves you, he will never tell you his deepest secret; he keeps it with God. If a man feels this way about women, why doesn't a woman feel that way about a man? A woman feels this way because she has a house and a home, but a man only has a house, which is his mother. If a man's mother is deceased and she did not buy a real estate house, then the son has no house, and is houseless for the rest of his life. Not only did he lose his only house, which is his mom, but she never bought a physical house to give him when she died. After her death, he is a homeless man, and a motherless child. He will only get a home through a mate, because his house is gone forever with God. Many women have been groomed to let a man take care of them, which destroys her independence. The expectations of women should be the same as the man when it comes to self-advancement. The reason a woman acts this way is because of the characteristic. A woman is territorial, and another woman is a threat to her house, which has a home, so one day she can have a family with her home. Due to the fact that a man has only a head, he gets his body from his mother, so therefore a man's only house is his mother's house, because he does not have a body. When a man leaves his wife or partner, he normally comes back to momma, his home. That is why a boy is called momma's boy and a girl is called daddy's little girl, because it is the brain who gave her life, not her mother brain. When you see another woman with a husband or serious partner, don't disturb her house looking for her home that she is building, so that one day they could have children and become a family. Let's break bread, goddesses, don't take that away from her. Find your own home, and one day you can have a child and you can live as a family. It is a fact that when a man leaves his home with you, you feel empty inside. Some people say go pray and go to church, or give your life to Jesus; in reality man is the electricity, and when he no longer desires you, but still in your house with you, not as your home, a woman dies on the inside. That is why it is best to utilize celibacy to find the man who really wants you, so you can enjoy your house with a home. A woman is territorial for this main reason. Many females have killed others, and some took their own lives due to this empty feeling that a woman feels. Some females can't sleep or eat. Some can't even date, and if they do, it takes them years to get over the man. Many woman will tell you, "I can't live without him." She would rather die. Goddesses, now that you know the truth, stop being submissive to a man; try being his wife. If he wants a submissive role, he should ask his kids to do that, not his wife. A submissive woman is frowned upon by other women. That's why it is best to take care of yourself. Don't be submissive. You are not a child, you are his home. Being submissive is a biblical lie, because all the days in the bible, women were not submissive and should not accept such abuse of language. To cure this deep down dying and abuse of power called submissive, find another home, or if you are single, you should never lie with a man without a gift called money, because if you invite him in your house, he might want to enter your home. If he enters your house to get to your home, and you did not get a gift, you are deemed unworthy, and you devalue yourself because he is man, the brain, born without a body. That is why he can skip to another home with grace, because he never had a house, which is a person's body. How can he respect your body when he never had a body? There are men who are not interested in marriage but only want to date or be in an uncommitted relationship with you. They are not promiscuous, but they will not respect your body unless you give and demand respect from men. It is up to the woman to decide her home after validation of the relationship. A woman's body is her house and her womanhood is her home. When a woman gets married, she turns her house into a home, and one day she will have children, and they will become a family who can reproduce in a harmonious way. In regard to religion, it was invented by man to blasphemy by God. Religion is a lifestyle, which are all in the occult world, because religion is a supernatural event to teach spirituality, to show man the proper way of living, and to set rules and guidelines about his family. The sacred atonement of a woman's body is physical supernatural. It is best to honor chastity over a man. Chastity is the best way to live your life until you find the right home for your house with acknowledgment called money. Let us live until we die. The end.

# The Decoding of the Bible

Genesis is the first book of the bible that tells of the world being built in seven days and the making of the human race. There is no way the universe could have been built in seven days, because it was a process to form the earth. The bible also stated that God rested on the seventh day. God does not rest; he is a spirit and does not require rest, which is a natural comfort for man, but not God. The main reason the seven days for the creation of man and world is not true is because the animals were here first. If man were made from the dust of the ground, then he would be first, but how did man acquire organs? Did God make each organ individually, or did he blow it into man with the breath of life, in order for man to become a living soul? The truth is, the DNA of man and dirt have no relations, so therefore man did not come from the earth, but was made to live on Earth, and to build and grown the universe. If man were made from dirt, then why can't this process be done today? The only way life can exist is through reproduction through a male and female. The reason for man's existence is to reproduce God as man with a female of its own kind. Own kind means the same kingdom; it does mean race. Here are some of the biblical stories that tells of incidents of the beginning of life on Planet Earth.

# Bereshit - In The Beginning

Based on the information in the bible, it states that the world was void and without life. The bible stated God created the world and man in seven days. How would you know if the world were built in seven days? There are no factual documents that revealed this information, other than hearsay from others. The world was not built for man; it was built for God, who so loved himself that he wanted to reproduce himself over and over again through reproduction. Reproduction of God is done through insemination of a man and woman. Planet Earth is over a trillion years old; it is impossible for anyone in the past life or this life to know anything factual about man during the beginning. Man does not know who he truly is or his purpose on Earth. The world was originally designed for gods and other spiritual beings unknown to man. Man by extinction is not as old as recorded. The process of life for man is different from animals; in order for man to exist, an animal conversion to human must be done, otherwise man would be like the primates, untrained and unsettled, due to the mind of the primate, which is considered dumb, but man has the mind of God which is the mind of a genius, to think and operate in a fashion to be considered a god. The only way man exist is through the animal kingdom with a god head. Man is a god. In order for God to walk on Earth as man, he created from a beast call a tiger, wild cat converted to a woman through sexual intercourse, and supernatural powers of Satan God. God made me because he wanted a companion to fill the Earth with man who is in the image of God, meaning man resembles God, and God is the father of the human race. I am the goddess of the world, born with supernatural powers given at conception and elevated at birth. Satan God so loved himself that he wanted to be multiplied throughout the world from generation to generation through man. There is a myth that Satan God walked on Earth as man. Satan God never walked on Earth as man; he is a spirit with different images. Lucifer, one of God's images, walked on Earth as God and man. Lucifer is a master at operating the spirit within you by teaching spirituality to the world, and giving aide to those that have grieved the spirit by their actions. The holy ghost is physical and is located at the base of all on Earth. This location is the home of the holy ghost who lies dormant. This mark of the beast, the serpent that is called the devil, is proof Satan is God. The reason many call the holy ghost the devil is because if you do not know how to operate your spirit, you can bring vexation to your soul. By learning how to live a civil life, you must do things that are civilized. The spirit of man is stronger than man, so if you do good things, it will magnify you; if you do bad things, it will get worst. If you are not careful, you can be led into some serious situations in your life. Let's take, for example, a man goes and kills his family, then he and the world blames the devil for his actions. To correct this person, his thinking must be rearranged by his thought patterns. He should embrace goodness instead of evilness. If he caters to evil, then he will do evil acts and because the spirit is stronger, he will be evil in thoughts and he will enjoy the evil act he committed, but if he communicates good things to the spirit, he will be a good man. Whatever you think you can be, and you believe that you can the spirit of God can make it happen. Man can only see God through a vision unless he reveals his image as the holy ghost or other images through a trance. The holy ghost is the first person in the trinity. The holy ghost is the physical being within you.

# The Afterlife for Man

In regard to the afterlife of man, which is a spirit transition, meaning another life on Earth living among the living. In the afterlife, the holy ghost will not remain with you but the feces will remain with you in the afterlife. The holy ghost is a living god. You have your own spirit that belongs to you. The mouth of the dead is full of feces because the holy ghost travels from the base of your spine and he settles in your mouth after death invisible to the naked eyes. The mouth is filled with feces which is the second life of the body. The reason death is a secret is because death is a thief, and a thief holds his tongue. There are misconceptions that man goes home to a long resting place; this is false information. When you die there is no rest because rest is earthly, not for the dead. All men are equal on Earth, but not in spiritual status. No woman is equal to a man. Man is life; without man you would not exist. All men came directly from God and woman came indirectly from God; in other words, woman came from a beast. The art of populating the earth cannot be done without a woman, because, I, Nora Goddess, am the first woman on Earth. In other words, a woman came on Earth before man, but man is elevated at conception because he is a god. All men were born without a body, so when he fathers a child, it is man who determines the sex of the male. Through the holy ghost, man receives a god head, heart, and his manhood, which is carried by the female because man has no body. There is one brain in man and two brain in a woman. The mind of a woman is an unsettled mind; that is why her thinking pattern is different from a man. All man carries a god head, which is located below man brain. The two brains indicate two minds which is a feature in humans being. The holy ghost is transferred to man during conception for this reason. A child is the bone of her bone and flesh of her flesh, giving the mother ownership of the child. A man is brain without a body. Without man, there is no life! If the brain dies, so will man. The man, which is called brain, and the body can live separately and can be transferred from one person to another through the death.

# The Reproduction System

The reproductive system of a man is his scrotum, which is located in the back middle of a man; that is why he cannot have children, because the scrotum cannot stretch like the uterus of a woman, plus his uterus is outside. It must be inside the body to produce life. There are misconceptions about children born with two organs. This is a birth defect. Only one of the organs usually function at its maximum capacity while the other is unusable. The organ that functions properly is the sex of the child. The operation should be done at birth. Mothers who let their kids carry both organs until they are old enough to is a mistake. The reason it is a mistake is because the child will be confused and ridiculed over this matter. The child will have identity problems and will require mental health. A mother is responsible for her children's decision making. This can be done at birth, and nobody has to know other than the doctor and his staff. In regard to the womanist, no child is born a womanist or manist, but can turn into a womanist or manist by choice, force, or lack of proper parenting. The spirit functions in unisex, meaning God is within male and female. The Christ-Constantine was a womanist, and a man who worked for God. If being a womanist were a sentence to hell, then he defeated hell. The acts gays do today is far more egregious than in past times. God judges a man by how he serves God; whether it is good or evil, it is man who represents God in him. The occult world has been vandalized by religious leaders who does not understand the spiritual world instead they write untrue information to sway others from learning the supernatural world. Man is spiritual in all fashion, but religion is a lifestyle; spirituality is your life. There is no cult in spirituality, but there is a cult in religion due to the bylaws they established and follow as a way of bonding with each other and agreeing on subjects that matter to all that is involved. No religious cult should ever denounce the spiritual world because the spirit is pure but religion is established. The occult world or spiritual world is sacred and holy, and it is wicked to imply that it is evil and hell is the home for they that practice the spiritual world. The spiritual world must be taught and supervised by holy men as well as wizards and sorcerer, and voodoo doctors. A voodoo doctor is a medical spiritual doctor. In regard to status, the religious world is for entertainment, but the spiritual world is a very sacred world and requires intense study and practice. The occult world needs to be very careful in selling products to others because the product could be used incorrectly and cause major havoc in a person's life or the life of that family. In the spiritual world, black magic and other magic need to be introduced to the world. The bible won't get you in heaven, but spirituality will. In the spiritual world, it is a sin to defame and lie on gods because you cannot see them but they are here on Earth. It is offensive to degrade gods in the religious world because you only know one world. The light! In order for a person to live to the fullest, he must live until he dies and never defame and say evil, ugly words about different religion, but in spirituality it is your mind body and spirit. A fool troubles his own spirit and a man who does not search his soul will find a book to find himself; that's why most people fail in the ministry because they use a book to determine their lives' goals and they let others make decisions for them, which the church or institution become an enabler to the person, but no comfort when they are in financial crisis for their members. Many ministers purchase a church based on membership, when in reality you should buy a church that you and only you can afford because members should not feel obligated to pay for your debts. God's word can be practiced anywhere, or if you wish to, you do not have to be religious. You can be a pagan, a non-believer, or a believer; the choice is yours. Being religious is a change in your lifestyle, and it should be a choice and not a standard obligation to a person. No one has to go to church or any institution to worship God; by worshiping yourself, you are worshipping God in your greatness, and if it is your greatness, then you made God part of your greatness, whatever it may be. Tithe and offering are your choice. God does not need money; he is naked and does not need money for anything. God has never seen a dime in tithe and offering, so why give your money in God's name? Give it in your name; you are the one who made the money, and you are the one who determines where you spend it. Be a man or a woman in your own house. The church is for entertainment, and if you want to pay the church bill and neglect yours, that's your decision. Spirituality is the way to develop oneself living in your mind, body, and spirit, which develops the fullness of the spirit. Why not be the captain of your soul while God drives the ship to dream the impossible dream and create an indestructible bond with the holy ghost/kundalini? He is God in the flesh. He that believes in himself believes in God. The goddess of the world.

# The ten commandments

Thou shall not steal means to take something of someone else with no intentions to return it. Why does a person steal? A person can steal due to jealously, low self-esteem social issues, proving independence, or a lack of respect for themselves and others. What is the profile of a thief? A thief is usually dexterous, stealthy, spying, picking locks, and can disarm things quickly. To help a person that steals, they need a character class or paladin, which is called a templar or crusader. A paladin should be knowledgeable about the thief act of 1968 to find out profiles of thieves and how to reinvent that person's lifestyle from thief back to his own good name.

Thou shall not lie means not to deceive others. When a person lies, he deceives himself, thus giving him a character flaw or flaws. To stop lying, accept yourself, don't make excuses for wrongdoing, and find out why you are lying, and is it necessary to lie in that given situation. If a person has a serious issue with lying, this is serious because lying is a complex situation, and if it is out of control, you may need the aid of a therapist to help you regain and rebuild your life from a belly filled with lies to an exhale of trustworthiness in your soul.

Thou shall not commit adultery means marital infidelity. The reason so many people commit adultery is because of the laws set up in marriage. First of all, marriage is a contract, and in a contract, it is binding on both partners. The major problem is that marriage is forever. The only thing that is forever is death, because no man has ever proven death wrong. Marriage should be in the increments of five years and renewable at the discretion of both parties. Many people stay in marriages due to religious reasons or what their belief systems are. Many people stay married due to financial reasons, some people stay married due to sickness of one partner, while others stay married due to convenience.

Thou shall love thy neighbor as thyself is to provide service and meet the needs of you and your neighbor. To pay your neighbor's debts is not your responsibility; your neighbor has a right to take care of themselves. How many people you know will pay their neighbors debt because they are having financial problems. To love thy neighbor as thyself simply means to respect your neighbors while respecting yourself. When you don't pay your debts, you are disrespecting yourself and bringing your character into question. The reason love thy neighbor as thyself does not work is because many people don't know or care to love themselves, and if they treat others better than they treat themselves, then they are hurting themselves and God. You must love yourself first. When you love you, you will do great things for yourself, and when you do great things for yourself, you just did a great thing for God, and if you want to share things with your neighbors, let it be your decision, not a decision of others. All decisions you make in life, you must always remember you are the one who will be living with the decisions you have made.

Thou shall love the lord thy God with all thy heart, mind, and spirit simply means to love you, because if you learn to love you, it will be easier to love God. If you cannot love yourself or the people around you who you can see and feel, how can you love God whom you can't see? The holy ghost is the physical being of God that is dwelled within your body at the base of your spine. The holy ghost is the mind, body, and spirit of God transferred to man, making man a god.

Thou shall have no other God before me simply means to honor God, first then all others come thereafter. A person's mother and father are Gods to a child. A husband can be a god to his wife. A pope is a god to man. A minister can be a god to his members. The problem is not who you consider a god, but always put the deity God before any other god, because Satan God is the maker of man, so therefore no man is higher than God or is equal to God, but man is God in earthly forms, because man is in the image of God.

Keep the sabbath day holy. The sabbath is celebrated on a day that is agreed upon by an organization. It is a day to cherish God and acknowledge his existence of man, and to give thanks for all of gods blessings to man.

Honor your father and mother. This is the only commandment that offers long life. A person who honors their mother and father is committing a holy act towards God, parents, and themselves. A parent is a god to their children, but you must teach them to love God first due to the order of respect to God.

Don't take the Lord's name in vain is called blasphemy. What is blasphemy? Blasphemy is the act or offense of speaking sacrilegiously about God or sacred things. It is profane to talk ill of the spiritual world, especially of God. The actions of the church to deliberately talk ill of God in the media or on tv teaches hate to the listeners. To tear down God's name not only is blasphemy; it is also grieving the spirit of God, which is a spiritual neglect of man towards God.

No graven images. What are graven images? Grave images are carved idols or representation of a god used as an object of worship. Graven images were the first signs of religion, because reading and writing were not invented yet. Paganism is one of the oldest religions; this is where religion began, and it will remain the one of the oldest religion. Through an idol, Christ was built, given life, and worshiped as a god, when in reality, Christ is a white man who operates to save the world from destruction of oneself and take care of the world as God has taken care of him.

# Biblical Terms

The serpent is called the holy ghost, the physical being of God. The holy ghost is also called the kundalini in the Hindu religion.

Two become as one means of the existence of male and female.

The trinity is the mind, body, and spirit; in other religions, it is the chakra.

God is everywhere, meaning the spirit within us, which is a live, supernatural entity.

Marriage means two people joining in a contractual agreement.

Holy reunion a is marriage between a man and a woman for the purpose of reproduction of man.

Nation means the ethnic group you were born into.

What are white people? The nation who represents God and Goddess.

What are black people? The nation who represents the Goddess and God.

World nation is all other nations on Earth that derived from the black and white nation to separate people by skin color instead of speech.

The devil is another name man calls God, and many call God this name in the image of the holy ghost.

The devil is an action that man commits that is not lawful or agreed upon, and is viewed as an unfit act.

God is a supernatural deity with different images and all images function differently.

A goddess is a deity or female human being.

The goddess is the mother of all on Earth.

Man is brain.

Brain is the life of the body; without brain, there is no life, but God is forever.

Woman/animal is the body of man and woman with an unsettled brain.

Lucifer is God as man on Earth. He is a spiritual advisor and the light of the world. He is an image of Satan God the deity. Pope Francis walks as God on Earth to bring man into unity with each other and God. Pope Francis shall also have a kingdom here on Earth and after life because he is worthy of the position, and he is not ashamed of God because of the misinformation that was given from centuries to centuries. Pope Francis shall be the one we name the keeper of the inheritance in this life and the afterlife. What is received on Earth will be received after death.

Virgin is a woman or man who has never engaged in a sexual act or a person who has not been sexually active for over ten years or more.

Gay men are men who have tendencies for the same sex. A gay man is called a womanist and a gay woman is called a manist.

Homosexuality in a male is sodomy which is the abuse of one's body and in many countries, it is a crime due to the nature of their sexual activities. To abuse oneself is an act of self-hate but it is hidden.

Born gay. No one is born gay but they can turn gay by force or choice. Although the spirit is in both man and woman, God is not in agreement with this form of sexual activities. God is not gay nor does he support it due to self-abuse called sodomy which is a crime that should be enforceable by law due to this destruction of the mind body and spirit.

Pope has elevated to godship; he has surpassed being a Christ.

Ministers are called Christ to teach and uphold the gospel between God and man.

Occult is the supernatural world man came from.

Where is God from? God is from the land of the dead.

Angels are supernatural spirits who speak to the human race.

Ghost is a deceased soul that can't be seen but can be felt and smelled.

Apparition is a spirit that can be seen, heard, or in some cases, both attributes in unusual circumstances

What is a demon? A demon is a god with powers. A demon can be a good spirit or a bad spirit. A demon is a person, place, or thing.

Satan the deity of the universe, which operates in different images but is considered one god.

Gifts are the abilities a person has that are supernatural.

Powers are for gods, not humans.

Death is a transformation from solid to air.

Afterlife is living in this world after death unseen, or living in Heaven or paradise

Manhood is in the form of the holy ghost weapon in a man, because man was born without a body.

Celibacy is to be without sex by mind force, which is not a guarantee.

Money is the root of all evil, or the love of money is the root of all evil. The correct version would be the lack of monies or the loss of money can be the root of some of your problems, allowing time to rebuild the mind energy and regain what was lost, and work toward abundance.

I make money, money doesn't make me. This statement should be reversed in wording. Money makes you, why, because with money you can make all of your dreams come true if want, desire, and plan to. You try and succeed at working to make money so that money makes you. Money makes you by establishing good credit which is viewed as one of your characteristics, and it is a system in America and other countries that is used to build trustworthiness. Credit reports can also be viewed negative toward that person, if even though that person is a wonderful, loving person, they don't pay their bills on time so they have a negative credit score, that can tarnish your character by negative information. To regain your character, start paying your debts on time and upgrade your credit score.

The American dream is to become credit-worthy so you can buy the things that you dreamed of having.

The devil made me do it is a somewhat correct statement if it is viewed in its entirety. A devil can't be a person, but it can be a place or thing that is challenged by who, what, when, where, why, and how to describe any situation. For example, a woman killed another woman or man. First, the spirit of God is a serpent, and the serpent is a beast god. The spirit overpowered her because she was living in evil, so therefore her spirit was living in evil because of your abuse of privilege with your mind not paying attention to the needs of the spirit, which is grooming and loving yourself, and building trust within you, which builds trust in the spirit. By using brain technique even though you are talking evil due to circumstances, you are not concentrating and focusing on a situation that would lead to who, what, when, where, and why. Who did the killing? A woman, who did she kill? She killed a man. Who was the man? Her husband. How did she kill him? She killed him with a knife; why did she kill him? Because she claimed she caught him with another woman. Who told her that? She heard it from a friend. What happened when the police and media arrived at the scene? She said to the media, "I need an attorney." When did this happen? One year ago. Where did this happen? Brazil. The who, what, when, where, why, and how should be used horizontally and vertically in finding the truth. For example, how could someone kill this man? Who is this man? Why kill him? Always use open-ended sentences or one word like how?

God is rich. How? No gods have needs for monies; they are naked and broke with supernatural powers.

Jesus was poor so that we may be rich. How? If he were poor, why would he give you when he had nothing for himself.? By definition, Jesus' plight in the bible is written in dictionaries as the description of a homeless man, which is categorized.

What is a narcissist? Gods and the human race?

Emotions? You were not born with emotions, only feelings. Emotions are functions of the brain that must be utilized by brainwaves. Here is an example of born with feelings. The reason a child screams at birth is the child is being squeezed, battered, choked, shortness of breath, hungry, climbing, and being pulled from an area that is too small to deliver children. The best practice is the c-section; no hole in your body cavity should be stretched and expect normality in a female. If you study cases of crimes and the birthing technique, you will notice that c-section children do much less crimes that vaginal birth, which sends the child body into havoc. Vaginal birth victims have a high history of crimes due to the abuse of vaginal delivery. Vaginal delivery encourages multiple birth, which is a major problem in the world. Overcrowded homes lead to homelessness and poverty, and the crime is rapid because you force false feelings on others. For example, if a person were completely honest with themselves, you will find that you don't care about anyone but you. If you learn to care about you, crime rate will drop because if you care, you would not do crimes that will place you in confinement. Let us take this a step further. Why should I care if my neighbor's lights are off and his car is broken? Seems like a personal problem. Why are his lights off? He is not working due to pandemic. Why did he spend all of his money and did not save for a rainy day? Why is he not going door to door to acquire work from neighbors? Why is he in bed after eight A.M.? Did he maintain his credit worthiness? How will he pay me back? I don't do handouts; I believe in closed fist, meaning be mindful of how you handle monies, because money has ears and it will fly away if you mistreat it, and it will come to you when you call it. You must stop using faith which are considered wishes in this situation. You are required to build your own future because only you have the map to your life to start building a financial future by means of work and education.

False me? False me is a person or nation who wants to be someone other than who they are. A pretender to themselves and the world.

The church and religious organization failed man.

The reason the religious organizations have issues is because they don't have an effective plan to handle the issues of the world; instead, they blame God for the problems of the world, when in fact it is man who misuses the power of the spirit of God called the holy ghost to commit crimes that cause man to suffer. The reason he commits crimes is because he does not harbor the severity of the crime. The reason he does not acknowledge the severity of the crime is because society has developed a plan to blame God for man problems. In order to cure this problem, you have to know the root of the problem. The root of the problem is baby! What is a baby? A baby is a full-grown man or woman who must grow into who they will become; who is responsible for the child's outcome? The parent or guardian. Case file #1: a child is born to a couple. A healthy male newborn. First, you have to research the biology of the infant. These are signs of hidden killers just to name a few they are 1. Broken bones, which can lower your self-esteem. 2. Loss of the sense of smell: without smell or taste, some of your sensory is lost because you need your five senses to function properly. The five senses are sight, touch, hearing, seeing and taste. 3. Broken sleep can alter your mood; it can cause irritability and anger

,which can cause you to ineffectively deal with stress and the issues that comes with stress. Trouble walking can be a sign of anxiety, which deals with the functioning of the brain. 4. Loneliness can lead to anxiety, depression, and suicide. 5. Instant need for money or other expensive items is related to anxiety and it is also a sign of unhappiness; it also shows that a person is not in control of their emotions, which can lead them to do things on impulse instead of thinking things over and resolving the issue at hand. 6. Low intelligence is a major problem, and it can be fixed but many people lack the knowledge to utilize self-help programs, and many will not go to a therapist due to negative feedback from others who might have had issues with a therapist. First of all, a baby is born without issues such as emotional act upon stress. They are born with feelings not emotions, but the stress is what needs to be handled. For stress of a crying child who is hungry is food and milk for an adult, it would be a different situation. Let's say this child is raised as killer or a murderer. Let us examine the child life of this person. How was he raised? Let's say he was raised in a household that had lots of problems getting along with his siblings or parents, who used a lot of verbal abuse and physical abuse on the child, along with neglect because the children spent a lot of time without their parents. The abuse was so severe that the child abused others by the time he was in grade school. During grade school, the child continued to act out by abusing other kids by hitting and other acts. The school have constantly sent letters home to the parent but to no avail; it was not resolved. The mother then takes the kid to another school to give the child a new start but the child exhibits the same behavior so the mother decides to work with the school to control his behavior, but she has the same problems. The mother then places the child in a program to interact with other students, but the child cannot adjust so they come up with a plan to deter the child's actions by punishing the child with no explanation or supervision to ensure the child follows the rules of the parent. There is no plan of punishment set aside for the child's behavior, nor or any rewards given to the child. This type of parent-child strategy is ineffective and it only frustrates the child, and he becomes a bigger problem in school. This is where the religious community takes action. The religious community should be skilled in the development of a child and should be concerned about the welfare of their members. There should be an intermission with the church and the parent of the child or family member. There should be law enforcement in place along with social services to help combat the problems of the family. In a situation like this, this act of the child is a character flaw. What is character? Your character is who you are by your thoughts, words, actions, and values. There are several character traits; here are a few of them: grit, self-control, optimism, zest, gratitude, and curiosity. If a person lacks these qualities, you must find out which character flaw the child exhibits and work on each flaw at a time, until the person becomes whole again or becomes deflawed for the first time in their lives. What is a character flaw? A character flaw is a deficiency in a person's personality that can bring on violent tempers and behaviors. A character flaw can add complexity to social interactions with others. There are three major types of flaws in a person's character. They can be minor, major, or tragic depending on the situation. Because a person's character is who they are, it is good to practice humanity because it leads to a good character. What is humanity? Humanity is to be passionate, generous, sympathetic, and learning to live together in harmony. What is harmony? Harmony is to maintain health and balance in life. In other words, harmony can change a person's life because it builds up the inner you, making your character harmonious. Many religious organizations can deter some of the violent crimes we have if they taught and preached the gospel for the betterment of man, not publicly criticizing God before the world when it is man who is committing acts of violence in the spirit, thus causing God to be criticized because of what you have done. Church should be a school of learning and worshipping. The church should have school for the poor in spirit to revive them and renew their spirits. In a church setting, the first hours should be for prayer and worshipping, and the second through fourth hour should be a classroom setting to teach humanity skills and have workshops to evaluate their knowledge of what they learned. There should be a program for church warriors to do home visits to families in crisis, and to help seek aid and funds for the department of social services. The church should build a financial fund program through the bank so the members can utilize the church assets by borrowing from the church and paying it back with interest. The church should also have a program for money management which can cause havoc in a person life due to the lack of it or having an abundance but not managed. The church should also teach their members about credit and the proper use of it, because borrowed monies will make you obligated to another person or institution ,but it will not make you a slave to that person, at least not in many countries. The reason the money should be paid back is to show independence and a willingness to care for oneself, and understanding that you must take care of yourself and be responsible by keeping a constant flow of monies in your bank account, which is called money management. The church should also provide housing for the homeless and the destitute, and help them regain financial status by helping them find jobs and homes. Many churches should be turned into housing for the disadvantaged and seek help through the government to help them pay for their housing at the church. The religious organizations should also be a part of the social services of their cities to help aide in the fight against poverty and other problems of the world. The church should also be teaching civilization. What is civilization? Civilization is the process by which society or a place reaches an advanced stage of social and cultural development and organization. To summarize this, the religious organizations should be symbolic to God, not against God. The religious and spiritual world represent God, whether it is good or evil. The world does not know God; if man did, he would know who he is, but he does not know who he is or the fullness of god. Religion is a lifestyle and spirituality is your life with your mind, body, and spirit.

# The set up of the church and other organizations:

Seven churches in one area of town.

**Examples:**

- First church is for all females of each nation learning to be a woman.
- Second church for all males of each nation learning to be a man.
- Third church ages five until 18 years old, different classes which are age appropriate .
- Fourth church housing for that city. Convert church rooms to apartments or boarding home.
- Fifth church alcohol and drug, murderers, child profilers with program funded by the state.
- Sixth church the banker for that city. Pooling all

monies together is lucrative and can build up a massive income for that city.

- Seventh church the fundraisers obtain jobs from business owners to help their business grow and building a profitable portfolio for the church and that city.

The fruit of the spirit is love, joy, peace, goodness, kindness, gentleness and self-control. These are all qualities of humanity. What is love? Love is deep affection, and deep affection is liking and caring for someone or something. What is joy? Joy is a feeling of pleasure and happiness. What is peace? Peace is concept of societal friendship and harmony without the presence of violence or hostility, what is goodness? Goodness is being good or virtuous. What is virtue? Virtue is living in a high moral standard. What is kindness? Kindness is being generous and considerate of others. What is gentleness? Gentleness is the act of being mild mannered, tender, and kind. What is self-control? Self-control is the ability to control oneself. What is oneself? Oneself is a person own self. These are the fruits of the spirit. The problem with the fruit of the spirit that is described in the bible and other documents are the same thing even though they are different words. In summary, they are seven fruits of the spirit that basically mean the same thing. The correct fruit of the spirit should be civilization, humanity, society, environment, law, spirituality, finance. What is civilization? Civilization is culture, society, and the way in which we live. What is humanity? Humanity is being compassionate, sympathetic, and the quality of your state of being. What is society? Society is living orderly in an orderly community. What is law? Law is a system of rules to regulate that city or country. What is spirituality? Spirituality is being concerned with the human soul or spirit instead of material or physical things. What is finance? Finance is to channel monies from savers to investors to entities that need them. The teaching and practicing of the new fruit of the spirit will rebuild man and give them a new start in life based on what he wants the outcome to be in his journeys in life. If a person lives life based on the new fruit of the spirit, he will live all of the fruits of the spirit listed in the bible, because in all of the new fruits of the spirit you have love, joy, peace, patience, goodness, kindness, gentleness, and self-control.

# The Revelation of Man

The book of revelations of the bible is not correct. The revelation is to reveal who man is. A baby is the bone of the bone and the flesh of the flesh of a woman. Woman came from me in the first life; beast converted to a woman, the creation of God, not man. All females carry the eggs for male and female. Due to the process of the human race, all men are born through a females and it is the male who determines the sex of the child. A female is born with the spirit because man was not born with a body, only a brain. The female transfers the holy ghost to her offspring. Who is man? Man is the brain, man is the life of the body, man is responsible for all functions of the body. Without man/brain, you would not be functional. The brain is the main system of the body. If the body dies, the brain can still live, but if the brain/man dies, death occurs. If the brain can be saved, it can be transferred to another body, and this man can be considered a living soul; in other words, he is brought back to life as a new man with the same body. The brain can also be recharged and reinstalled, but the brain must be kept in an incubator. There are many who have prosthetic legs and other artificial body parts; patients can receive pure flesh by removing body parts from the dead to reinstall on another person. It is true that the entire human body can be replaced by the body parts of the dead. There is no reason to let great body parts rot in the grave when man can use his extremities to save another person's life, because he won't be needing it anymore. In order to do this to make donating body parts official, there must be a section on documents at the DMV for donations of organs; it should now be read body parts and organs. In regard to blood, the blood can be used in medicine to help with medical issues that are present in the world. In regard to burial, it is a choice, but sea burial is better because it will feed the animals of the ocean. Burial is a choice that takes up land spaces and it is an unnecessary procedure because you are having the funeral for you, not the dead; it is costly and gives false feelings of endearment. The major question is who is man? Man is the force of life, he is the brain, he has the god head and passes it to his offspring, converting a dumb animal mind into a highly intelligent human mind called genius. Man is a force of energy for life to exist and function. The trinity is mind/brain which is man, the god head, the genius. The holy ghost which is the spirit and manhood for man because man does not have a body, but he has a heart and his manhood from the holy ghost; he is the weapon located in man as the penis. The body, which is the female flesh of my flesh and bones of my bones, makes up the trinity. The spirit the holy ghost who is Satan God in the physical form as a serpent located at the base of mankind is called the holy ghost. Being taught God takes care of man, that statement is not true; it is man who takes care of God. You as a human being take care of God by providing things for yourself. Whenever you do good in life for yourself, you did the same for God. God give thanks to man for the great things man has done for himself, he also did it for God. If a man buys a new home, then God has a new home. If a man buys himself an island, then God has an island. If a man becomes rich, he pleases God because God is now rich. If a man remains poor, then God remains poor, but is thankful for what you received because God received it also. If a man lives in a shack, then God lives in a shack; in other words, it is man who takes care of God and it is God who made man and the world for man to inhabit. All forces of the universe are controlled by us. Volcanos are evil acts of nature; they can only be destroyed by us, but they are not of us; they came in from the ground. Man is not able to control or destroy these forces because he is not Satan; man has the spirit of Satan, but Satan is my god. Satan is God and he is the deity of the world; no mythologic god comes before God; in fact they take instructions from God. Satan has many images and all function differently to assist man. There is a myth that man came from the dust of the ground, and that Lilith and other false gods were here first. This is untrue. If man came from the dust of the ground, then man belongs to the volcanoes for they are the only spirits that came from the ground, and they are evil spirits here to destroy man. They are invisible because they don't know me. The law you just pleased God. The church is not set up correctly when it comes to giving monies. A church should never give away monies but loan it with a definite plan for a person to pay it back. A church should be run by the minister, but it is ran by the members; that's why it is important for you to own your own church with your own ability to pay for it. Religion is a lifestyle; why not have a bank account for your church? You are the messenger; why not get all of your monies and if they need monies let them borrow from you with or without a credit check? The choice is yours. A church should be talking about how to improve one-self, not devil. You are God. Remember it was man who named God the devil.

Yet as Christians and Catholics, you are very good at helping others; in fact, I praise you for all the great things you have done, yet it was done in vain, because if it were blessed, poverty would be fixed. Man has de-feated himself by not caring for himself first, but caring for others more than he cares for himself, because many were taught to give your last if someone needs it. Many religious people are living a lie; they help others and are sitting in their homes hungry and broke, but giving to others to show you care. In reality, you care for others more than you care for yourself and this makes a person aloft with himself, which is abuse of thy self. Why would you give someone your last when the last is all you have? If you do this act, it means you don't love yourself as much as you love others. The bible and its contents have ruined the lives of many by choice; many people know Jesus is a myth, but they have been lying so long that it hurts them to seek the truth because a lie does not hurt; it only hides a person's passive aggressive behavior. You will be able to control oneself. A passive aggressive person has serious issues and they don't know it. There are many self-help books out there, but if a therapist is available, they would be more suitable for you, because you must remember as Christians and Catholics you are passive aggressive due to your misunderstanding of the teaching.

# Who was Jesus Christ?

Jesus Christ is a myth of a god. Jesus as he is stated in the bible could not be a man because of the events. Take for example Jesus walking on water. Due to the scientific facts of weight, a person would sink even though water is solid and liquid. There is no man on Earth who can walk on water or defeat death. In order for a person to walk on water, he must be in the afterlife and their feet will not touch the water due to the loss of life. Due to the nonexistence of dirt/earth to stabilize your life, is it also means a something or someone vile, mean, or worthless. Dirt is also an unclean matter. Dirt is earth or soil, which is the dry surface that makes up Planet Earth. Dirt is also considered the brown stuff on the ground. Why would God make man from filth? What are ashes? Ashes are pulverized bone fragments. Ash by definition is the solid, powdery substance that is left over after any fuel undergoes combustion. The human body is mainly composed of water, carbon, and bones. The idea that man came from dirt is false because who was yesshuraa, yesshurah, yeshura, Jesus?

Yesshurah is part of our third set of children. None of our children had supernatural powers because it is not for men but for gods. God gave Yesshuraa' the second nation to populate the earth as man, which is the white nation, which is also God's nation in tone. During Yesshuraa' time he defied his father by not wanting to advance mankind by skin tone. He began to practice black and white magic to compete with his father. He allowed his children to commit homosexuality, let you honor him, and his father is here on Earth; this would be a vile act against his father who he knows raised him in spirit, and so can his step-children whom he held in his hands while in my womb. Can tell you God raised them by spirit? My mortal husband can tell you God is in his house. Always remember sometimes the light can fool you into the truth and in some cases it can lead you into darkness; that's why you must utilize who, what, when, where, why, and how, then at the end of the survey, the truth will be revealed. Is my world God gave and no man will ever make me feel unwelcome in my house.

Tolerate me even if you don't want to. Celebrate me when I decide I want to go home. Why should I go back home when God is here with me? We are married and we have a son in this life, also guess what, I don't have a day of death and that is called everlasting life. We are here to represent the truth about God and man. Nation, the lost nation, the hidden nation that man doesn't want you to see. I would like to introduce you to our son and his sisters, God's step-children, who will represent the biracial nation on Earth. Our son will never own eyes. All nation on Earth belongs to Satan God and Nora Goddess. The British and the Americans are the only nation of Yesshuraa; in other words, the British and the Americans are our first grandchildren of our eldest son, Yesshuraa'. The world call him Jesus. All nations were made by all of our other sons and daughters. In other words, all of our sons have their own nation, so therefore you would never find Yesshuraa in the Middle East because he was born into the British nation and they would have never ventured into each other's nation, because mixing of the race was not allowed in those times. Be careful of what you promise God, because he will require this of you, so be clear in your speech to God. Be clear in your speech to God because it is your speech that can awaken the spirit, and this act is a violation of

God if you did not receive it through spirituality. To use any type of witchcraft to awaken the spirit is death. The reason so many people who have awoken the spirit are sick is because you did not get it honestly; you got it through the shining of the teeth to believe you will be gods and that you will have great powers. The great powers you will have are great pain. Yesshuraa' was right in his devil, yet he did devilish acts against his father, God. The broken bond between father and son is the reason people think there are two gods: a good god and an evil god. God is not evil; this is an act of man. After Yesshura defied God, God made his own nations, and each son was over that nation which can be viewed to this day. Italy, Cuba, and so forth. There is no person on Earth who has ever seen God walk on Earth in the flesh as man; he only walks in the spirit as he does in me today. God cannot be seen but his powers can be witnessed by man. The spirit within man is stronger than man, so be careful what you ask God to deceive another. We loved all of our sons. I have no bad feeling about Yesshuraa' and Africa, even though they did his family wrong. Yesshuraa' crucified his father in word and his nation crucified him in the physical form, then lied that our son from the Jewish nation, crucified him by nailing him to the tree, and saying forgive them for they not know what they have done. This is not true. Yesshuraa's children said this to God after they killed their father. Yesshuraa' acted like a devil; he was not a devil because there is no such entity as a devil whom was given the name by Yesshurra' calling his father the teeth. Many people have lost their fortune by the shining of the teeth; many people were trafficked to other countries by the showing of the teeth. Many people have made themselves look rich when they were poor by the showing of the teeth. Many families have ruined one another by the showing of the teeth. This is a deceitful act and should be abolished; it is an act that have many people in jail and in their graves by the showing of the teeth. Many people develop mental issues due to the direct deceit of another person that can cause another person to stumble and fall. A smiles should be sincere, not forced to him with shining teeth and good words which deceived him and ultimately caused his death. Yesshuraa' was a man, not a god, but a great man. To honor a man over God is a sin when you know the truth, because Yesshuraa' is not God. In other words, he died as he lived in a smile of deceit by the same sword he taught his nation, and that sword stands to this day and has ruined many people's lives due to this false tactic, smiling to show you are kind, when in fact, some are raving wolves. This tactic of the showing of the teeth is so dangerous that many people have lost their lives to people they know by the showing of choice of protein. Free gifts have made man poor by his own decisions and the way in which he lives. To give someone something free is preparing a person for failure. There is nothing wrong with worshiping Yesshuraa' or any other man, but to take the name of God and smear it to the world in lies is wrong, and you know that it is wrong. To defame God to the world is teaching hate, evilness, and all the negativities that go with gossip. The tongue is evil and Yesshuraa' used an evil tongue against his father. He lived by the sword and he died by the sword, smiling to show kindness with a smile, and his children killed blacks needed to hear, plus there were gifts! In order for the black nation to build their nation, they must eliminate weed, food stamps, and welfare, and determine as a nation who you are going to be, and not let other nations dictate to you who you are. You are the sons and daughters of God and Yesshuraa's nation is of the son of a mortal man, so therefore you let your brother children stand over you by choice. Many modern-day Africans are Christians due to gifts such as free food and other items, which is not the way a person should live. Why give them food when you can give them seed and cattle, or they're not going to buy or own slaves anymore. If they did, they would be just like the Asians and the Palestine nations who own slaves to this day, and the blacks still support them even though they know they own slaves, but are making a lot of fuss about their forefathers who were slaves 400 years ago in the USA, yet they don't try to free the slaves they see now, but are fighting for the ones who have died. Anyone who is Catholic or Christians or any nation who believe that Jesus is God is worshiping man and not God; that's why they say you have to come by the son in order to get to the fathers, and this is all many Africans first came to the USA. They were supposed to follow the Jewish nation, but through gifts they defied the Jews and gravitated to Yesshuraa' nation even though this is the nation that defied them and caused other nations to defy them through lies and treatment. The black nation depends on others to build their nation, when in reality, Africa had jewels that would have made them some of the richest nation on earth but they follow others instead of leading their own nation. Africa sold his own people and is selling them now; the reason Africans can't get along with Britain is because Great Britain does, and in other countries, they are given gifts that enable them not to advance due to getting something for nothing, which resulted in the nation depending on Yesshuraa's nation, and openly living a lie to show honor to their brother and his children, while neglecting his own and worshipping his brother's children instead of his own, due to the color of the skin. To this day, Yesshuraa's children and the black nation are fighting over skin color, hair texture, and looks, while the vast majority of the world is worried about how to support their families and how to live with respect towards one another. When they preached the undecoded bible, any nation and all that joined in religious ranting and raving about God is also defying God by defaming God in his own world, so that the mortal son could stand before his father, but it is impossible because Yesshuraa' was a man, not a God, and no man can defeat God. The black nation Africa our son sold his birth rights through the shining of the teeth and his stomach. To be full blooded, only people of the same nation by blood are full blooded of that nation. The black nation is a very large nation, but they allowed Yesshuraa' and his children to rule over them due to gifts. In the USA, they have the highest crime rate in the world because they defy humanity and civilization by the treatment of other nations. The British/Americans are the only nation of Yesshuraa, God's oldest children are the grandchildren of God. A nation that worships God does not worship homosexuality and other acts that is detrimental to mankind. There is no one who can tell you who to love but you should love in kindness to yourself. In today's world you will find fathers against sons and mothers against daughters which is more pronounced in Yesshuraa' and the black nation and all who because he is invisible. Yesshuraa and Africa had lots of problems with his children. Yesshuraa' had two sons; one was smooth and one hairy. Yesshuraa' one son murdered the other. Africa also had sons who gave up their birth right, also had two sons. One son stole; the other son birthright through his mother who showed favoritism towards her children. Everything Yesshuraa' and Africa said about his father, he and his children did. In the nation of Yesshuraa' homosexuality was practiced during those times and is still practiced and worshipped today. In Yesshuraa' nation on the religious side of their endeavors they are five feet deep with stones on the top of his gravesite. When you move the stones, it will reveal his burial place. Before his sons killed him, he asked his sons, "Why have thou forsaken me?" then they covered him up alive. His body is buried next to a tree that has writing on it in English. Yesshuraa was considered a devil by the things he said and did. He abhorred good and evil, not his father, Satan. God is a spirit. He can't be seen, so who did all these things like lying, stealing, commit adultery, backstabbing, and a host of lies about God? It was Yesshuraa' and Africa who did these things that could be seen. If God did these things, it would not be seen, because God was with me as you see him in this life. My children never saw God; if they did, it was only in a dream, but his presence was always with us. God is a spirit/angel, so Yesshuraa felt that he should have my powers because he is a man, while my other children obeyed me and were sensitive about their fathers, who made them rich through ideas, and they protected me because it was the duty of the sons to revere their mother. When Yesshuraa' was a middle-aged man, Yesshuraa' was never seen again. He left with his brother africa and five of his sons. This is the location of Yesshuraa' body he is in a hole. We honor our son in this life to represent the biracial nation which many live in the slums, the forgotten children of the world that were thrown away, so God took them back. Yesshuraa' was a crusader but he did not have a solid financial foundation. Fundraising and asking for money is a form of begging which teaches man how to rely on each other instead of every man for himself and God for us all. Yesshuraa called me woman because my name was woman, but Itty named me Nora, and the name was agreed upon. Yesshuraa did not mention me often, because he defied me also getting free food and monies from the government, and started, utilizing some of those funds to the slum areas by upgrading those houses or home improvement, or building apartment flats for them. Many of them have good credit or no credit, because where are they spending it on it is definitely not in the housing department. Many of these people could purchase homes that have been on the market for a long time. In order to solve this problem, you must first solve the major problems. First, we must bring the countries into a debt-free status; then they can revise the financial industry and allocate funds where stamps needs to be revised, because this hidden act of kindness has kept many people poor with filled stomach and shining teeth and eyes accepting the notion that they must do the same thing the next day look for the enabler, who is actually a burden, not a savior. There is a world that really needs help to get on their feet, and those are the people who lives in the slums of our world, a world the media hides, and a world that the church and other religious places avoid, because the poverty is so great it looks like a hopeless situation, but it is not. To fix this problem, you need to reevaluate the people who are currently love themselves first, then others. The black nation needs to be independent of all nations because they don't need the help as much as other nations who actually have a major disadvantage, such as severe disability or a condition that would allow them to be unemployable. In the black and some of the Hispanic nations, they suffer from inertia which can be mastered by going to work and taking care of yourselves. Depending on others to take care of your financial problems is a sure way to fail in life because you are here to care for yourself, not depend on other nations to pick up the slack. Welfare and food only the ones who mixed the race are biracial; they are really from the African nation, but are considered black due to the respect of the Egyptians to honor another nation. The only ones that are black are the ones that had relations with the black nation, but they are not black people. In regards to acceptance, there is no other nation on Earth that will beg another nation to accept them as human beings and then marry them. The black nation needs to start taking proper care of their nation and stop depending on your brother children to offer to support to you. The black nation must join together as a nation and look at the other whites such as the Jewish nation, the Cubans, the Mexicans, the Asians, the Egyptians, and so forth, They look like the descendants of the Jewish nation because the Jewish nation has different facial features and tone, which are obvious when you look at the people of the world. Yesshura's children look different than our white children; that's how you will know the difference. Look at them! The Jewish nation has different levels of white because we had three sets of twins in the Jewish nation. Many people believe that the Jewish and the Egyptians are black. The Jewish nation and the Egyptians are white, always the right way, even if it were wrong. Every bad act on Earth was done by Yesshuraa' his children and the black nation. The black nation is the only nation on Earth that begs for another nation to be with them and accept them. The black nation would marry into a nation that declares dominance over them, yet they are your brother children and you are the children of God. The black nation is always in competition with the whites and there is no reason for it because the whites from England are also the Americans. They are not of God, but of the son. If you don't believe it, take a look at the British and Americans. This is a false statement and should be abolished from the minds of man. In regards to slavery, Africa had a slave mentality; he sold his inheritance through his eyes and stomach. Through, gifts he, his wife, and children worshipped his brother Yesshuraa' and his brother kids. In fact, he treated his brother children better than he did his own, because he was convinced his skin was less valuable than his brother. Yesshuraa' always took care of Africa while he begged for his family and people. Yesshura always had superficial wealth because he wanted to get it from others to benefit him. Yesshuraa's way was son, a mortal man, not the father. In the Christian and Catholic religion, it is written that Christians and the Catholics say you must come through the son to get to the father. They knew that the son was not God, but respected the son more than the father and led the world into false belief about God. Nobody has to rely on another person to come to God; this is your privilege to pray to God. You can come to God on your own because the spirit of God lies dormant in some and awake in many. This statement was made to give Yesshuraa' power over all man, and if you did not know Yesshuraa', you will not meet God. It is important to remain your children's parents and never allow them to be your friends, because one day they may treat you as a friend. There was a long list of verbal abuse towards God. Yesshuraa's lies that were used against God stood as lies all these years. The media was a great way to finish teaching the world hate for a man the world does not know. Invented Yesshuraa' children went to the media and took God's name and ruined it through lies of their father, but now the world will witness the truth when they unearth Yesshuraa'. Let the world know that when you worship Yesshuraa', you are worshipping the sons; then told others that his father brother, the Jew, killed him and hung him on a tree, but it never happened. Even to this day, Yesshuraa's children and Yesshuraa's children continued what their fathers started; they continued to defame God, believing in man and notGgod. The holy bible is an undecoded document. Yesshuraa' did not want any other nation on Earth except his, and this was not God's plan, so God made his own nation and took the rights to fill the Earth as far as the eyes could see from Yesshuraa'. God saw that a son will compete against a father if he is a friend; that is why it is children of God's and not the children of God. The Jewish nation are the chosen ones because they are the first nation of the father, not the son. It is important in parenting your children you should remain a parent to your children and not be a girlfriend or boyfriend to your children, because this form of parenting usually backfires as the child grows older in age and maturity. Yesshuraa' was a friend to his children, and as a result, they took their father's life, threw him in a hole, and covered it with stones to rid him of the world without a trace, but only in memory; at least, that's what they intended. Fish and the bread, which is a statement in the bible that Jesus fed a multitude of people with bread and twelve fish. The people ate ground birds which later were called chickens. After all God had done for Yesshuraa', he continue to defame his father to his children and his children's children, and as a result, God made his own nation of whites called the Jewish nation. The Jewish nation populated the Earth, not Yesshuraa'. Yesshuraa' defied God and therefore his nation did not grow; the whites from England and America are the off-spring of Yesshuraa, the grandchildren of God; that is why they are called him. He did not have powers, so he invented witchcraft and the occult world, which were used for good deeds, not bad deeds. Take, for example, twelve fish and a basket of bread called manna. This is a false statement. First of all, manna are birds. There is an old saying, which came first, the chicken or the eggs? The correct answer would be the eggs because the chickens are the birds that could not fly, so they fell from the skies and people ate them, bred them, and chicken became a living ground meal for man. If the men of the bible had twelve fish, I can tell you without a doubt in my mind that he and his sons ate the hear. He told you lies and what person on Earth can identify him stealing things. What prison on Earth ever jailed God the Almighty, who is Satan God? The spirit of God is embedded in man as a serpent to let man know that he is always with man. God makes man aware of the things to come through touch of the nerve sensory or through vision. Why would God hurt man when he so loves himself that he wanted to make man in his image so that man can be a testament to God, not a debunk of God? Yesshuraa', our son, was a man with no powers; the only powers he had were the ones that were performed by God through the doctor, the lawyer, the police, the judge; he is everything to man. If man knew God's description, why are there so many pictures of devils? You call God, in reality the devil is the mind of man; it is the mind that rules over man, so if man does not operate his mind correctly, he can be dysfunctional. The book also states God was wrestling all night with a man. God does not wrestle with men as men do with each other. God wrestles with men in a spiritual way, not a physical way. The bible and many documents states that God is liar, thief, and he does evilness to man. How is God a liar and a thief, and how can you prove it? You can't. How can that be true? Who saw God with a woman in the flesh in any book? The truth is God is here, there, and everywhere; he is the inner serpent that resides in all on the earth. The spirit is the one who will tell all that you have done in your life upon death. He is the sixth sense, or in some cases, they call it the middle eye, which simply means using common sense. The six sense is stronger; you can even hear his voice, or many see God in a vision, but no man on Earth has even seen Satan God in the flesh, because he is a spirit. He can't be seen, not even in the afterlife. In the afterlife, he is only heard, never seen. He is the healer; he is God made in the image of a black man. He is of the father, not of the son, so therefore the whites from Britain and America are the first grand on Earth not the first sons and daughters. It is a blessing that God has grandchildren; what a glory hallelujah. God is a deity/angel, not a human being ;he does not need black magic, voodoo, or any other man-operated tricks. Tricks are for men! God is the power! Let us now examine some of the untruth about God. Jesus is God; Jesus is a myth and he is not God. If there were a Jesus, he would be god son. The religious book states that God has a woman, a very good blessing from God, so he wanted to take the blessing from God and have men honor him. So God made his own nation of whites called the Jewish nation to replenish the earth in his name. Yesshuraa' was disobedient towards his father. If man doubts this, look at the whites from Britain and the American whites, and you will see that their whitish appearance is different from all the other whites on Earth. Even though Yesshuraa's nation was born first, he is second to God. No son comes before his father, no matter what he achieves in life. Africa/Satan God the father of the black nation whom same room or country. In modern day, rough drafting should be done by a trained professional; this is not a do-it-yourself project; it is a do it for yourself project. In the beginning, mental illness was cured by white magic by the man you call Jesus? White magic and plants of the earth were used as healing methods for illnesses. In the beginning magic was a preferred method that many people used and by using these magic and portions Yesshuraa' and his mate marry wanted to rule the world, but Yesshuraa' had no powers, only magic. After Yesshuraa' and Mary had children, they saw that this was the beginning; the proper method of blood transfusion was the drinking of the blood, but they had developed methods to make a machine that would infuse the blood. In modern day, there are many people who suffer with mental illness, which can come from poor eating habit and your lifestyle, but some do need the help of a professional, but many needs to take care of the wellness of their body, mind, and spirit. In the beginning, we used a rough draft to eradicate mental illness. A rough draft is an unfinished document that the brains can communicate with each other even when they are not, in which is a violation for mankind and is a sure way to meet death, which is a thief. Homosexuality was started by Christians and it is still practiced in Christianity and Catholicism to this day. There is a great myth about the bible, and I am going to tell you the correction in the myths. The bible is about God and his sons. I was not mentioned by my sons who called me woman. None of my children ever saw their dad, but he walked in me then as he does now. It is evident that God is with me due to my supernatural powers, separate from the powers of god. There is a lot of wording in the bible about the blood of man.

# The characteristics of Satan God

**Independent-** the ability to be strong and able to survive alone.

**Responsibility-** the ability to act independently and make decision without authorization.

**Liability-** the decision to be responsible for your actions.

**Unity-** the ability to join together as one.

**Promote-** the art of advancing oneself in life opportunities.

**Education-** moral, intellectual, and social instruction to others.

**Craftiness-** to work or have a trade.

**Common sense-** to make good and sound judgment.

**Law-** to abide by a system of rules.

**Finance-** management of your money.

# The Holy Ghost/Kundalini

The holy ghost is not the evidence that Satan is the maker of man and all living things in the universe. The holy ghost is the mark of the beast which is a supernatural physical God described as the king cobra, which is at the base of your spine. The spirit of this God is dominant, but He is not asleep. I was born with the holy ghost and remained with Satan as my god, but not to this day. The holy ghost is also called the kundalini, which is a Sacred God and should not be grieved. Here is a description of the holy ghost and my actual encounter with this God. The physical spirits within on November 2018, I was looking at the tv and suddenly I could not move. My stomach felt like it was filled with broken glasses. The glasses were very sharp, but I did not feel any pain. Then I felt the serpent enter my insides; then I looked up at the tv and I saw the spiritual God as a serpent. He stuck his head out of my right shoulder and he had a big smile on his face. He had beautiful jewels across the top of his forehead. He has full lips on the bottom and thin lip on the top. He has long, stainless steel feeling fangs on each side. After the spirit showed himself to me, he went back into my body and began to move throughout my body. This God is a man serpent, the king cobra who is the holy ghost. He performs as a man in all manners. He is the greatest lover in this world and the supernatural world. Do not tempt him! The holy ghost is the only image of God that smiles, the holy ghost also speaks in a human voice and he speaks all languages. There have been many books published making false claims that the holy ghost/kundalini is a female, which is absolutely false. Why would Angel God create the human race and give another God the credit! Many people claim that they have bad experiences with the kundalini holy ghost, because man does not know who God is. If you are having a bad experience, it is evident that you are grieving the Spirit of God. There are no human beings on Earth that can remove the holy ghost from your body; if they told you they can, they told you a lie, and you will find that their claims are unfounded. A person who receives this great gift should honor all aspect of their lives. The holy ghost will lead you to the truth, even if the truth hurts. To thy own self be true because everyone has good and evil in them; it is the one you embrace is the one that will be the strongest. In other words, it is you who determines your actions in life, it is you who magnify you or defeat you, it is you who chooses to live on Earth in Heaven, or you can live your life in Hell on Earth by your own actions. It is your life, and you should live your life to shine, not darkness. Your spirit at the base of your spine is the spirit of Truth. Upon death, it is the holy ghost who will tell all that you have done in your life on Earth. There are many instructors who instruct you on the kundalini. Don't be fooled; this is a serious matter. A live snake will enter your body and moves around 24 hours a day, seven days a week, and there is not one day you will not feel his presence. Many people who are not prepared are living a life that they are not happy with. Many complain about the nonstop tugging and pulling sensations. Some people are having mental issues due to the holy ghost. The church did not prepare man for the Spirit of God, because they he did not know the true god. Man has been fooled by the church and other authors about a false god called Jesus. Many believe God is a dove, which is outrageous. The image of God as a bird; he is a birdman. I have him on print the face of a rare bird, but he is a man in features. The truth is the snake that is at your base of your spine; man called the devil, in other words, you are devilish, which is an act to do evil. The choice is yours. Live your life until you die. Do not die in your life while living.

# The Passover- over 100 attendance

The synagogue had a Passover diner to celebrate the Jewish nation. When I arrived, the room was filled with people. I was placed at the last table at the front with other members and guests. I was sitting across from a mother and daughter. Who attended the event? We began to talk about the Jewish culture and where to get kosher foods. I told them it was best to go to a Jewish butcher to prepare the meat. We began to talk about religion and the daughter asked me, "How can someone be a Christian and Jewish?" I told the daughter that the Christians follow the bible to the fullest, especially the older ones. I told the young lady that when I was growing up, the white women did not believe in having children out of wed lock. Then I started to look for something in my purse. I scooted down in my chair, and then while I was looking for something in my purse, the young lady said to me, "What religion are you?" I asked her if she were serious, she said yes. The Spirit of God rolled around in the seat, and that's when the monster entered inside me. I heard the sound of four hooves moving back and forth like a huge horse; he was massive in size. He turned his buttock to my right side, then he pushed his body inside mine. As he was entering my body, my blood was covering his body, my blood was gushing like a waterfall. When he was completely inside of me, I felt his warm body inside mine. Then He adjusted his wide eyes, which are very wide like a dinosaur. I felt electricity flowing throughout my body. He focused his eyes on the young lady and stared at her in an angry way. Then he looked at her mother, then he turned back to the daughter. The daughter placed her hand over her mouth and her eyes were wide and terrified, and her mother looked at me in a blind stare. They were both in shock. I felt and saw electricity coming from my finger. He moved my head back and forth. He began looking at the people next to me. Then He looked to the side, then he looked behind me with his head moving up and down in a fast motion. When His eyes focused on the altar, he took my neck in a single motion and turned back to the initial position facing the woman and her daughter. God then took my fingers and was hitting it on the table in dissatisfaction. I heard Him giggle like a white female. God placed my head on the table over my two hands crossed, and placed my head to the left, facing the wall. I was asleep.

Approximately two weeks later, He showed me what he did. When God performs in my body, I am in a trance.

At the ceremony for my baptism, which was performed by the rabbi, they had to catch my legs because my body was floating in the air.

At the synagogue, He took my fingers and wrote to the rabbi of an event that the members were about to do to him while he was out of town.

At the synagogue, the rabbi stated to me on many occasions that it was unusual for me to speak Arabic and I could pronounce it as if I studied the language.

The rabbi performed the ceremony for God to walk on Earth as man.

# Satan God as Man/Lucifer

Satan God in the image of man is slightly different from humans. Satan has no sclera; instead, his eyes are entirely black/gray with tiny, bright stars in his eyes. God's eyes are the eyes of God, the light of the world. Satan is a very tall man, approximately 6'7 or taller. He has large feet and large hands that look like size 16 or larger. Satan is a muscular deity with beautiful, jet-black hair. He has thin lips in this image, the same lips as man. Satan has a big, gray, moonlight surrounding. His head, he is naked, and his feet are as fine brass. When God walks, his walk echoes. When God walks, it sounds like he is walking on a thick glass that echoes as he walks. Satan is a beautiful man with a blind stare. God is the ultimate ruler, and all knees bow to him. Death does not exist for angels.

# At the Cross

Here is one of my encounters with Satan in our bed-room. One night, I was awakened by Satan; he was lying between my legs, staring at me. Satan is so beautiful that I was speechless at his beauty. I could not speak. The light around his head looked like the brightness of the gray moon; it was directly centered at the back crown of the head. He is approximately 24 to 25 years old because he is forever young. While Satan looked into my eyes, I saw that he was in love with me but I did not know what to do or how to respond to him. At that time, I realized a man loves with his eyes. I was so overcome with shock that Satan closed my eyes. When I woke up, I could not stop telling Satan how beautiful he is and how much I love God and adore him. On June 11th, man was placed on Earth. The next secret of God is death;

no man has ever defeated death. The next secret is life. No man can create life, but he can give everlasting life to a robot. The next secret is God head. No man will ever know God as he knows another man, because God is the deity. No man is equal to God and no son is equal to his father. No matter what the son acquires in life, he will always be considered his father's son or sons or daughters.

# Satan God as the Tiger God

Satan God as a tiger is in the image of a tiger with the face of God as man. God as the tiger. God is buck skin brown with a very long, seductive tail. He wears a short haircut with three razor lines on the left side of his head. God in this image is a young man. My experience with God in this life is very interesting. One night while I was lying in my bed, I was awakened by a growling sound followed by movements under my cover. At the bottom of my bed, God was crawling on his four legs on his stomach. God crawled to the top of my bed, then he sighed and turned his head towards the window, which is located to my right. He did not look directly at me, but from the side view, I could tell he was unhappy about something. I did not ask him what was wrong; I just laid in my bed, then I went to sleep. The second time he came in my bed, he was lying on top of me with his large paws on my breasts, gently squeezing them. I was not afraid but I was amazed why I did not feel the full weight of his body because he is a large tiger. After my experience with God, I went to sleep.

Cloud face god.

# Satan God as the Cloud Face God

Satan God is the ruler of Heaven and Earth. All forces on Earth are the force of god. In the image of the cloud face God, he is encircled in the clouds as the cloud face God. His image is of the Middle East nations. God has a full beard. His hair is white like the clouds, and he has a blind stare. Here is my experience with Satan as the cloud face God. One morning, I was in my bed daydreaming when God placed me in a trance. I saw God with a blind stare hovering over my bed; he was sucking my body up towards his mouth with a strong wind force coming from his mouth. His jaws were filled with air. God made love to me, then I woke up out of the trance. In this image as the cloud face God, he does not have a body in this image; only his face encircled in the clouds. Many religious people have placed clothing of different styles on God, but the truth is, God is naked. Where is God going to get clothing from? Where is he getting the money from? God does not have an earthly job from nine to five. What would be the purpose of God wearing clothes and spending monies? God is a spirit, and he does not wear clothing, nor does he have any money nor does God need yours. God through his spirit can tell you how to make money by directing your thoughts to develop a plan to build wealth and to enjoy a pleasurable life on Earth. Here is my example of building wealth. I have paid $240,000 on my home loan, yet the house only cost $109,000 18 years ago. My plan for wealth is to rent my upstairs apartment at $1,200.00 per month and rent my third unit for $700.00 per month. This amount of monies will give me passive income of $22,800 per year. In five years, I will accumulate $114,000.00; in ten years, I will have $228,000.00. God is taken care of by man, so if you don't prepare yourself for success, you have already failed in life. God is the force in man; man is the force that drives the force within him. Without God, there is no man; without man, there is no life on Earth.

# Satan God as the Storm God

Satan God as the storm God is a huge ball of dark storm clouds with a face of an Indian man. One night, I was placed in a trance in a foreign land in Asia. There was a huge storm during the day hours when a strong wind began to destroy the land in that area. There were a lot of small Asian children hiding from the storm under bushes and behind houses for protection. I looked up, God looked back at me, and he stared at me, but I was not afraid. I was not afraid because I felt that I was a part of this spiritual event. When God looked at me, his eyes were piercing. In the image as the storm God, his eyes are not completely black; in this image he has a cornea. God controls all forces on Earth, and storms are a part of the Earth forces, and are necessary for life on Earth and the formation of the land. Climate change is also a part of the maintenance to enforce and abide by to control hazards in the world. Pollution and other man-made issues can be controlled, but the weather can only be forecast or predicted, but no man can claim that he can control the natural forces of the world. Man can build dams, but severe storms can destroy dams and entire areas due to its forces, which cannot be controlled. Storms literally shape the form of the Earth; they are a part of a continuous change in weather conditions. Storms are considered evil to man, but it is this evil that helped form Planet Earth. Storms are considered to be evil; to man, it is evil, because man is accustomed to normal weather, but hurricanes, tornadoes, and other major disasters are considered the glory of the earth. The reason so many people fear these weathers is because buildings and other structures lack the requirements to withstand the forces of nature. Today's structures are not as solid as many of the structures built in ancient times and other eras. In today's world, people build houses for looks instead of safety. Some buildings are built on unstable grounds with proper land analysis compromised because their clients value beauty over safety. Many destructions of buildings can be prevented if they were built on solid foundations. If infrastructure is not maintained properly, it will deteriorate and cause havoc during different storms. The bottom line is to build for safety, not beauty. The material used today is modern, but it is not safe. Houses should not be made of wood, but of stone, bricks, and barriers to protect the land from the oceans.